MW00511775

All Things New

All Things New

*Transforming Promises
from the Word of God*

Revell

a division of Baker Publishing Group
Grand Rapids, Michigan

© 2010 by Revell

Published by Revell
a division of Baker Publishing Group
P.O. Box 6287, Grand Rapids, MI 49516-6287
www.revellbooks.com

Printed in the United States of America

ISBN 978-0-8007-7178-2 (pbk.)
ISBN 978-0-8007-1930-2 (cloth)

Scripture is taken from the King James Version of the Bible.

10   11   12   13   14   15   16   7   6   5   4   3   2   1

God promises us new life and reminds us of our "born again" status again and again—in his Word and through his work in the world.

But it is hard to *feel* new when we wake up in the same "old" bodies, surrounded by our past mistakes. They travel with us from day to day, and Satan loves to use those visible elements of our life to keep us from discovering the reality of God's work in our lives—that step by step, choice by choice, we are becoming a new creature.

Let's face it. We all need constant reminders of who we are in Christ. Day by day, hour by hour, we are in need of God's sustaining truth about what he has done—redeemed our souls and our lives—and what that means for us—a new day, a brand new life!

We've gathered together over 250 passages from Scripture into this volume to do just that. Slip it into your bag, keep it by your bed. Share it with a friend. And may God use it to clothe you in the new identity he's created for you.

And God saw every thing that
he had made, and, behold, it
was very good.

Genesis 1:31

Wherefore I say unto thee,
Her sins, which are many, are
forgiven; for she loved much:
but to whom little is forgiven,
the same loveth little.

Luke 7:47

It is God that girdeth me
with strength, and maketh
my way perfect.

Psalm 18:32

It is of the LORD's mercies that we
are not consumed, because his
compassions fail not.

They are new every morning:
great is thy faithfulness.

Lamentations 3:22–23

For ye are dead, and your life
is hid with Christ in God.
When Christ, who is our life, shall
appear, then shall ye also appear
with him in glory.

Colossians 3:3–4

I will call upon the LORD,
who is worthy to be praised:
so shall I be saved
from mine enemies.

Psalm 18:3

Cast away from you all your transgressions, whereby ye have transgressed; and make you a new heart and a new spirit: for why will ye die, O house of Israel?

For I have no pleasure in the death of him that dieth, saith the Lord GOD: wherefore turn yourselves, and live ye.

Ezekiel 18:31–32

Stand fast therefore in the liberty wherewith Christ hath made us free, and be not entangled again with the yoke of bondage.

Galatians 5:1

Hast thou not known? hast thou
not heard, that the everlasting
God, the LORD, the Creator of
the ends of the earth, fainteth
not, neither is weary? there is no
searching of his understanding.

He giveth power to the faint;
and to them that have no might he
increaseth strength.

Even the youths shall faint and
be weary, and the young men shall
utterly fall:

But they that wait upon the
LORD shall renew their strength;
they shall mount up with wings as
eagles; they shall run, and not be
weary; and they shall walk, and
not faint.

Isaiah 40:28–31

Come now, and let us reason together, saith the LORD: though your sins be as scarlet, they shall be as white as snow; though they be red like crimson, they shall be as wool.

Isaiah 1:18

The LORD is the portion of mine inheritance and of my cup: thou maintainest my lot.

The lines are fallen unto me in pleasant places; yea, I have a goodly heritage.

Psalm 16:5–6

Blessed be the God and Father of our
Lord Jesus Christ, which according to his
abundant mercy hath begotten us again
unto a lively hope by the resurrection of
Jesus Christ from the dead,

To an inheritance incorruptible, and
undefiled, and that fadeth not away,
reserved in heaven for you,

Who are kept by the power of God
through faith unto salvation ready to be
revealed in the last time.

1 Peter 1:3–5

For the LORD is good; his
mercy is everlasting; and
his truth endureth to all
generations.

Psalm 100:5

But exhort one another daily,
while it is called To day; lest any
of you be hardened through the
deceitfulness of sin.

Hebrews 3:13

Arise for our help,
and redeem us for thy
mercies' sake.

Psalm 44:26

Though he fall, he shall not be
utterly cast down: for the LORD
upholdeth him with his hand.

Psalm 37:24

Remember ye not the former
things, neither consider the
things of old.

Isaiah 43:18

Therefore if any man be in Christ,
he is a new creature: old things are
passed away; behold, all things are
become new.

2 Corinthians 5:17

The LORD also will be a refuge
for the oppressed, a refuge in
times of trouble.

Psalm 9:9

In all thy ways
acknowledge him, and
he shall direct thy paths.

Proverbs 3:6

I, even I, am he that blotteth
out thy transgressions for
mine own sake, and will not
remember thy sins.

Isaiah 43:25

He that findeth his life
shall lose it: and he that
loseth his life for my sake
shall find it.

Matthew 10:39

Blessed be God, which hath
not turned away my prayer,
nor his mercy from me.

Psalm 66:20

The Spirit of the Lord GOD is upon
me; because the LORD hath anointed
me to preach good tidings unto the
meek; he hath sent me to bind up the
brokenhearted, to proclaim liberty to
the captives, and the opening of the
prison to them that are bound.

Isaiah 61:1

Jesus said unto her, I am the
resurrection, and the life: he that
believeth in me, though he were
dead, yet shall he live:
    And whosoever liveth and
believeth in me shall never die.
Believest thou this?

John 11:25–26

When Jesus had lifted up himself, and saw none but the woman, he said unto her, Woman, where are those thine accusers? hath no man condemned thee?

She said, No man, Lord. And Jesus said unto her, Neither do I condemn thee: go, and sin no more.

Then spake Jesus again unto them, saying, I am the light of the world: he that followeth me shall not walk in darkness, but shall have the light of life.

John 8:10–12

Cast thy burden upon the LORD, and he shall sustain thee: he shall never suffer the righteous to be moved.

Psalm 55:22

The LORD is merciful and
gracious, slow to anger, and
plenteous in mercy.

Psalm 103:8

How excellent is thy lovingkindness,
O God! therefore the children of
men put their trust under the shadow
of thy wings.

They shall be abundantly satisfied
with the fatness of thy house; and
thou shalt make them drink of the
river of thy pleasures.

For with thee is the fountain of life:
in thy light shall we see light.

Psalm 36:7–9

For, behold, I create new heavens and
a new earth: and the former shall not
be remembered, nor come into mind.

Isaiah 65:17

Therefore being justified by
faith, we have peace with God
through our Lord Jesus Christ.

Romans 5:1

Search me, O God, and
know my heart: try me, and
know my thoughts:
  And see if there be any
wicked way in me, and lead
me in the way everlasting.

Psalm 139:23–24

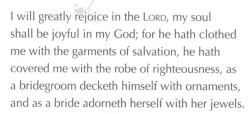

I will greatly rejoice in the LORD, my soul
shall be joyful in my God; for he hath clothed
me with the garments of salvation, he hath
covered me with the robe of righteousness, as
a bridegroom decketh himself with ornaments,
and as a bride adorneth herself with her jewels.

Isaiah 61:10

But as for me, I will come into thy house in the multitude of thy mercy: and in thy fear will I worship toward thy holy temple.

Lead me, O LORD, in thy righteousness because of mine enemies; make thy way straight before my face.

Psalm 5:7–8

The LORD thy God in the midst of thee is mighty; he will save, he will rejoice over thee with joy; he will rest in his love, he will joy over thee with singing.

Zephaniah 3:17

Blessed is he whose transgression is forgiven, whose sin is covered.

Blessed is the man unto whom the LORD imputeth not iniquity, and in whose spirit there is no guile.

Psalm 32:1–2

And it shall come to pass, that
whosoever shall call on the name
of the LORD shall be delivered: for in
mount Zion and in Jerusalem shall be
deliverance, as the LORD hath said,
and in the remnant whom the LORD
shall call.

Joel 2:32

For the Son of man is
come to seek and to save
that which was lost.

Luke 19:10

I acknowledge my sin unto
thee, and mine iniquity have
I not hid. I said, I will confess
my transgressions unto the
LORD; and thou forgavest the
iniquity of my sin.

Psalm 32:5

After this manner therefore pray ye: Our Father
which art in heaven, Hallowed be thy name. Thy
kingdom come. Thy will be done in earth, as it is
in heaven. Give us this day our daily bread. And
forgive us our debts, as we forgive our debtors.
And lead us not into temptation, but deliver us
from evil: For thine is the kingdom, and the power,
and the glory, for ever. Amen.

Matthew 6:9–13

Have not I commanded thee?
Be strong and of a good
courage; be not afraid, neither
be thou dismayed: for the
Lord thy God is with thee
whithersoever thou goest.

Joshua 1:9

And he took the cup, and gave thanks, and gave it to them, saying, Drink ye all of it;

For this is my blood of the new testament, which is shed for many for the remission of sins.

Matthew 26:27–28

And they that know thy name will put their trust in thee: for thou, LORD, hast not forsaken them that seek thee.

Psalm 9:10

Know therefore that the LORD thy
God, he is God, the faithful God,
which keepeth covenant and mercy
with them that love him and keep
his commandments to a thousand
generations.

Deuteronomy 7:9

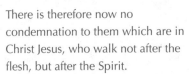

There is therefore now no
condemnation to them which are in
Christ Jesus, who walk not after the
flesh, but after the Spirit.

For the law of the Spirit of life in
Christ Jesus hath made me free from
the law of sin and death.

Romans 8:1–2

Likewise the Spirit also helpeth our infirmities: for we know not what we should pray for as we ought: but the Spirit itself maketh intercession for us with groanings which cannot be uttered.

And he that searcheth the hearts knoweth what is the mind of the Spirit, because he maketh intercession for the saints according to the will of God.

And we know that all things work together for good to them that love God, to them who are the called according to his purpose.

Romans 8:26–28

I say unto you, that likewise
joy shall be in heaven over one
sinner that repenteth, more
than over ninety and nine
just persons, which need no
repentance.

Luke 15:7

I sought the LORD, and he heard
me, and delivered me from all
my fears.
    They looked unto him, and
were lightened: and their faces
were not ashamed.

Psalm 34:4–5

The thief cometh not, but
for to steal, and to kill, and
to destroy: I am come that
they might have life, and
that they might have it more
abundantly.

John 10:10

(For the LORD thy God is a merciful God;) he will not forsake thee, neither destroy thee, nor forget the covenant of thy fathers which he sware unto them.

Deuteronomy 4:31

Likewise, I say unto you, there is joy in the presence of the angels of God over one sinner that repenteth.

Luke 15:10

Verily, verily, I say unto you, He that believeth on me hath everlasting life.

John 6:47

Therefore we are buried
with him by baptism into
death: that like as Christ
was raised up from the
dead by the glory of the
Father, even so we also
should walk in newness
of life.

Romans 6:4

Teach me thy way, O Lord; I
will walk in thy truth: unite my
heart to fear thy name.

I will praise thee, O Lord
my God, with all my heart:
and I will glorify thy name for
evermore.

For great is thy mercy toward
me: and thou hast delivered my
soul from the lowest hell.

Psalm 86:11–13

Blessed be the LORD: for he
hath shewed me his marvellous
kindness in a strong city.

For I said in my haste, I am
cut off from before thine eyes:
nevertheless thou heardest the
voice of my supplications when I
cried unto thee.

O love the LORD, all ye his
saints: for the Lord preserveth the
faithful, and plentifully rewardeth
the proud doer.

Be of good courage, and he
shall strengthen your heart, all ye
that hope in the LORD.

Psalm 31:21–24

Repent ye therefore, and be
converted, that your sins may
be blotted out, when the times
of refreshing shall come from
the presence of the Lord;

And he shall send Jesus
Christ, which before was
preached unto you.

Acts 3:19–20

Blessed is the man whose
strength is in thee; in whose
heart are the ways of them.

Who passing through the
valley of Baca make it a well;
the rain also filleth the pools.

They go from strength to
strength, every one of them in
Zion appeareth before God.

Psalm 84:5–7

Thou hast turned for me my mourning into dancing: thou hast put off my sackcloth, and girded me with gladness;

To the end that my glory may sing praise to thee, and not be silent. O LORD my God, I will give thanks unto thee for ever.

Psalm 30:11–12

Then will I sprinkle clean water upon you, and ye shall be clean: from all your filthiness, and from all your idols, will I cleanse you.

Ezekiel 36:25

To him give all the prophets witness, that through his name whosoever believeth in him shall receive remission of sins.

Acts 10:43

Knowing this, that our old man is crucified with him, that the body of sin might be destroyed, that henceforth we should not serve sin.
For he that is dead is freed from sin.

Romans 6:6–7

Behold, the former things are come to pass, and new things do I declare: before they spring forth I tell you of them.

Isaiah 42:9

And he hath put a new song in my mouth, even praise unto our God: many shall see it, and fear, and shall trust in the LORD.

Psalm 40:3

And if ye be Christ's, then are ye Abraham's seed, and heirs according to the promise.

Galatians 3:29

Then shalt thou understand the fear of the LORD, and find the knowledge of God.

For the LORD giveth wisdom: out of his mouth cometh knowledge and understanding.

Proverbs 2:5–6

The LORD is my light and my salvation; whom shall I fear? the LORD is the strength of my life; of whom shall I be afraid?

Psalm 27:1

That ye put off concerning
the former conversation the
old man, which is corrupt
according to the deceitful lusts;

And be renewed in the spirit
of your mind;

And that ye put on the
new man, which after God is
created in righteousness and
true holiness.

Ephesians 4:22–24

The LORD openeth the
eyes of the blind: the LORD
raiseth them that are bowed
down: the LORD loveth the
righteous.

Psalm 146:8

Likewise reckon ye also
yourselves to be dead indeed
unto sin, but alive unto God
through Jesus Christ our Lord.

Romans 6:11

There be many that say,
Who will shew us any good?
LORD, lift thou up the light of
thy countenance upon us.

Thou hast put gladness in
my heart, more than in the
time that their corn and their
wine increased.

I will both lay me down in
peace, and sleep: for thou,
LORD, only makest me dwell
in safety.

Psalm 4:6–8

Blessed be the LORD, that hath
given rest unto his people
Israel, according to all that
he promised: there hath not
failed one word of all his good
promise, which he promised by
the hand of Moses his servant.

1 Kings 8:56

I am crucified with Christ:
nevertheless I live; yet not I, but
Christ liveth in me: and the life
which I now live in the flesh I
live by the faith of the Son of
God, who loved me, and gave
himself for me.

Galatians 2:20

For the LORD taketh
pleasure in his people:
he will beautify the meek
with salvation.

Psalm 149:4

Is any among you afflicted? let him pray. Is any merry? let him sing psalms.

Is any sick among you? let him call for the elders of the church; and let them pray over him, anointing him with oil in the name of the Lord:

And the prayer of faith shall save the sick, and the Lord shall raise him up; and if he have committed sins, they shall be forgiven him.

Confess your faults one to another, and pray one for another, that ye may be healed. The effectual fervent prayer of a righteous man availeth much.

James 5:13–16

Cast not away therefore your
confidence, which hath great
recompence of reward.

For ye have need of patience,
that, after ye have done the will
of God, ye might receive the
promise.

For yet a little while, and he
that shall come will come, and
will not tarry.

Now the just shall live by
faith: but if any man draw back,
my soul shall have no pleasure
in him.

But we are not of them who
draw back unto perdition; but of
them that believe to the saving
of the soul.

Hebrews 10:35–39

Shew me thy ways, O LORD; teach me thy paths.

Lead me in thy truth, and teach me: for thou art the God of my salvation; on thee do I wait all the day.

Remember, O LORD, thy tender mercies and thy lovingkindnesses; for they have been ever of old.

Remember not the sins of my youth, nor my transgressions: according to thy mercy remember thou me for thy goodness' sake, O LORD.

Psalm 25:4–7

O Lord, thou art my God;
I will exalt thee, I will
praise thy name; for thou
hast done wonderful
things; thy counsels of old
are faithfulness and truth.

Isaiah 25:1

For sin shall not have
dominion over you: for ye
are not under the law, but
under grace.

Romans 6:14

I will instruct thee and
teach thee in the way
which thou shalt go:
I will guide thee with
mine eye.

Psalm 32:8

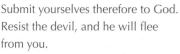

Submit yourselves therefore to God. Resist the devil, and he will flee from you.

Draw nigh to God, and he will draw nigh to you. Cleanse your hands, ye sinners; and purify your hearts, ye double minded.

Be afflicted, and mourn, and weep: let your laughter be turned to mourning, and your joy to heaviness.

Humble yourselves in the sight of the Lord, and he shall lift you up.

James 4:7–10

Yea, I have spoken it,
I will also bring it to
pass; I have purposed
it, I will also do it.

Isaiah 46:11

What shall we then say to these things? If God be for us, who can be against us?

He that spared not his own Son, but delivered him up for us all, how shall he not with him also freely give us all things?

Who shall lay any thing to the charge of God's elect? It is God that justifieth.

Who is he that condemneth? It is Christ that died, yea rather, that is risen again, who is even at the right hand of God, who also maketh intercession for us.

Who shall separate us from the love of Christ? shall tribulation, or distress, or persecution, or famine, or nakedness, or peril, or sword?

As it is written, For thy sake we are killed all the day long; we are accounted as sheep for the slaughter.

Nay, in all these things we are more than conquerors through him that loved us.

For I am persuaded, that neither death, nor life, nor angels, nor principalities, nor powers, nor things present, nor things to come,

Nor height, nor depth, nor any other creature, shall be able to separate us from the love of God, which is in Christ Jesus our Lord.

Romans 8:31–39

The LORD is my shepherd; I shall not want.

He maketh me to lie down in green pastures: he leadeth me beside the still waters.

He restoreth my soul: he leadeth me in the paths of righteousness for his name's sake.

Yea, though I walk through the valley of the shadow of death, I will fear no evil: for thou art with me; thy rod and thy staff they comfort me.

Thou preparest a table before me in the presence of mine enemies: thou anointest my head with oil; my cup runneth over.

Surely goodness and mercy shall follow me all the days of my life: and I will dwell in the house of the LORD for ever.

Psalm 23

Being confident of this very thing, that he which hath begun a good work in you will perform it until the day of Jesus Christ.

Philippians 1:6

I have set the LORD always before me: because he is at my right hand, I shall not be moved.

Therefore my heart is glad, and my glory rejoiceth: my flesh also shall rest in hope.

For thou wilt not leave my soul in hell; neither wilt thou suffer thine Holy One to see corruption.

Thou wilt shew me the path of life: in thy presence is fulness of joy; at thy right hand there are pleasures for evermore.

Psalm 16:8–11

But now being made free
from sin, and become servants
to God, ye have your fruit
unto holiness, and the end
everlasting life.

For the wages of sin is death;
but the gift of God is eternal life
through Jesus Christ our Lord.

Romans 6:22–23

I will be glad and rejoice
in thy mercy: for thou hast
considered my trouble;
thou hast known my soul in
adversities;

And hast not shut me up
into the hand of the enemy:
thou hast set my feet in a
large room.

Psalm 31:7–8

Now unto him that is able to keep you from falling, and to present you faultless before the presence of his glory with exceeding joy,

To the only wise God our Saviour, be glory and majesty, dominion and power, both now and ever. Amen.

Jude 24–25

The righteous cry, and the LORD heareth, and delivereth them out of all their troubles.

The LORD is nigh unto them that are of a broken heart; and saveth such as be of a contrite spirit.

Many are the afflictions of the righteous: but the LORD delivereth him out of them all.

Psalm 34:17–19

That Christ may dwell in your hearts by faith;
that ye, being rooted and grounded in love,

May be able to comprehend with all saints
what is the breadth, and length, and depth,
and height;

And to know the love of Christ, which
passeth knowledge, that ye might be filled
with all the fulness of God.

Now unto him that is able to do exceeding
abundantly above all that we ask or think,
according to the power that worketh in us,

Unto him be glory in the church by Christ
Jesus throughout all ages, world without end.
Amen.

Ephesians 3:17–21

But God be thanked, that ye
were the servants of sin, but
ye have obeyed from the heart
that form of doctrine which was
delivered you.

Being then made free from
sin, ye became the servants of
righteousness.

Romans 6:17–18

The steps of a good man are
ordered by the LORD: and he
delighteth in his way.

Though he fall, he shall not
be utterly cast down: for the
LORD upholdeth him with his
hand.

I have been young, and now
am old; yet have I not seen the
righteous forsaken, nor his seed
begging bread.

Psalm 37:23–25

But God hath chosen the foolish things of the world to confound the wise; and God hath chosen the weak things of the world to confound the things which are mighty;

And base things of the world, and things which are despised, hath God chosen, yea, and things which are not, to bring to nought things that are:

That no flesh should glory in his presence.

But of him are ye in Christ Jesus, who of God is made unto us wisdom, and righteousness, and sanctification, and redemption.

1 Corinthians 1:27–30

For to be carnally minded is death; but to be spiritually minded is life and peace.

Romans 8:6

Because he hath set his love upon me, therefore will I deliver him: I will set him on high, because he hath known my name.

He shall call upon me, and I will answer him: I will be with him in trouble; I will deliver him, and honour him.

With long life will I satisfy him, and shew him my salvation.

Psalm 91:14–16

I can do all things
through Christ which
strengtheneth me.

Philippians 4:13

When mine enemies are
turned back, they shall fall
and perish at thy presence.
For thou hast maintained
my right and my cause; thou
satest in the throne judging
right.

Psalm 9:3–4

Behold, I will do a new
thing; now it shall spring
forth; shall ye not know it? I
will even make a way in the
wilderness, and rivers in the
desert.

Isaiah 43:19

For which cause we faint not;
but though our outward man
perish, yet the inward man is
renewed day by day.

For our light affliction, which
is but for a moment, worketh
for us a far more exceeding and
eternal weight of glory.

2 Corinthians 4:16–17

For thou, LORD, wilt
bless the righteous; with
favour wilt thou compass
him as with a shield.

Psalm 5:12

For he is our peace, who
hath made both one, and
hath broken down the
middle wall of partition
between us.

Ephesians 2:14

God is our refuge and strength, a very present help in trouble.

Therefore will not we fear, though the earth be removed, and though the mountains be carried into the midst of the sea;

Though the waters thereof roar and be troubled, though the mountains shake with the swelling thereof. Selah.

There is a river, the streams whereof shall make glad the city of God, the holy place of the tabernacles of the most High.

God is in the midst of her; she shall not be moved: God shall help her, and that right early.

The heathen raged, the kingdoms were moved: he uttered his voice, the earth melted.

The Lord of hosts is with us; the God of Jacob is our refuge. Selah.

Come, behold the works of the Lord, what desolations he hath made in the earth.

He maketh wars to cease unto the end of the earth; he breaketh the bow, and cutteth the spear in sunder; he burneth the chariot in the fire.

Be still, and know that I am God: I will be exalted among the heathen, I will be exalted in the earth.

The Lord of hosts is with us; the God of Jacob is our refuge. Selah.

Psalm 46

And they sung a new song,
saying, Thou art worthy to take
the book, and to open the seals
thereof: for thou wast slain, and
hast redeemed us to God by thy
blood out of every kindred, and
tongue, and people, and nation

Revelation 5:9

Many are the afflictions
of the righteous: but the
LORD delivereth him out
of them all.

Psalm 34:19

A new heart also will I give
you, and a new spirit will
I put within you: and I will
take away the stony heart out
of your flesh, and I will give
you an heart of flesh.

Ezekiel 36:26

But if the Spirit of him that raised
up Jesus from the dead dwell
in you, he that raised up Christ
from the dead shall also quicken
your mortal bodies by his Spirit
that dwelleth in you.

Romans 8:11

For thou wilt light my
candle: the LORD my God
will enlighten my darkness.

Psalm 18:28

And many people shall go and say,
Come ye, and let us go up to the
mountain of the LORD, to the house of
the God of Jacob; and he will teach us of
his ways, and we will walk in his paths:
for out of Zion shall go forth the law, and
the word of the LORD from Jerusalem.

Isaiah 2:3

Know ye not that ye are the temple of God, and that the Spirit of God dwelleth in you?

1 Corinthians 3:16

Behold, the Lord G OD will help me; who is he that shall condemn me? lo, they all shall wax old as a garment; the moth shall eat them up.

Isaiah 50:9

Though I walk in the midst of trouble, thou wilt revive me: thou shalt stretch forth thine hand against the wrath of mine enemies, and thy right hand shall save me.

Psalm 138:7

Put on therefore, as the elect of God, holy and beloved, bowels of mercies, kindness, humbleness of mind, meekness, longsuffering;

Forbearing one another, and forgiving one another, if any man have a quarrel against any: even as Christ forgave you, so also do ye.

And above all these things put on charity, which is the bond of perfectness.

Colossians 3:12–14

The LORD is good, a strong hold in the day of trouble; and he knoweth them that trust in him.

Nahum 1:7

Wherefore the law was our schoolmaster to bring us unto Christ, that we might be justified by faith.

But after that faith is come, we are no longer under a schoolmaster.

For ye are all the children of God by faith in Christ Jesus.

For as many of you as have been baptized into Christ have put on Christ.

Galatians 3:24–27

But know that the LORD hath set apart him that is godly for himself: the LORD will hear when I call unto him.

Psalm 4:3

Brethren, I count not myself to have apprehended: but this one thing I do, forgetting those things which are behind, and reaching forth unto those things which are before,

I press toward the mark for the prize of the high calling of God in Christ Jesus.

Philippians 3:13–14

Thou hast also given me the shield of thy salvation: and thy right hand hath holden me up, and thy gentleness hath made me great.

Thou hast enlarged my steps under me, that my feet did not slip.

Psalm 18:35–36

The Spirit itself beareth witness
with our spirit, that we are the
children of God:

And if children, then heirs;
heirs of God, and joint-heirs with
Christ; if so be that we suffer
with him, that we may be also
glorified together.

Romans 8:16–17

And the God of peace shall bruise
Satan under your feet shortly. The
grace of our Lord Jesus Christ be with
you. Amen.

Romans 16:20

The Lord redeemeth the soul
of his servants: and none of
them that trust in him shall
be desolate.

Psalm 34:22

He sent from above, he took me, he drew me out of many waters.

He delivered me from my strong enemy, and from them which hated me: for they were too strong for me.

They prevented me in the day of my calamity: but the LORD was my stay.

He brought me forth also into a large place; he delivered me, because he delighted in me.

Psalm 18:16–19

For the mountains shall depart, and the hills be removed; but my kindness shall not depart from thee, neither shall the covenant of my peace be removed, saith the LORD that hath mercy on thee.

Isaiah 54:10

And be not conformed to this world: but be ye transformed by the renewing of your mind, that ye may prove what is that good, and acceptable, and perfect, will of God.

Romans 12:2

Thou art my hiding place; thou shalt preserve me from trouble; thou shalt compass me about with songs of deliverance. Selah.

Psalm 32:7

A man's heart deviseth his way: but the LORD directeth his steps.

Proverbs 16:9

Now thanks be unto God,
which always causeth us
to triumph in Christ, and
maketh manifest the savour
of his knowledge by us in
every place.

2 Corinthians 2:14

Sacrifice and offering thou didst
not desire; mine ears hast thou
opened: burnt offering and sin
offering hast thou not required.
Then said I, Lo, I come: in the
volume of the book it is written
of me,
I delight to do thy will, O my
God: yea, thy law is within my
heart.

Psalm 40:6–8

I thank my God always on your behalf, for the grace of God which is given you by Jesus Christ;

That in every thing ye are enriched by him, in all utterance, and in all knowledge;

Even as the testimony of Christ was confirmed in you:

So that ye come behind in no gift; waiting for the coming of our Lord Jesus Christ:

Who shall also confirm you unto the end, that ye may be blameless in the day of our Lord Jesus Christ.

1 Corinthians 1:4–8

I will extol thee, O LORD; for thou hast lifted me up, and hast not made my foes to rejoice over me.

O LORD my God, I cried unto thee, and thou hast healed me.

O LORD, thou hast brought up my soul from the grave: thou hast kept me alive, that I should not go down to the pit.

Sing unto the LORD, O ye saints of his, and give thanks at the remembrance of his holiness.

For his anger endureth but a moment; in his favour is life: weeping may endure for a night, but joy cometh in the morning.

Psalm 30:1–5

Now the Lord is that Spirit: and where the Spirit of the Lord is, there is liberty.

But we all, with open face beholding as in a glass the glory of the Lord, are changed into the same image from glory to glory, even as by the Spirit of the Lord.

2 Corinthians 3:17–18

And thine ears shall hear a word behind thee, saying, This is the way, walk ye in it, when ye turn to the right hand, and when ye turn to the left.

Isaiah 30:21

The steps of a good man are ordered by the LORD: and he delighteth in his way.

Psalm 37:23

Wherefore thou art no
more a servant, but a son;
and if a son, then an heir
of God through Christ.

Galatians 4:7

I had fainted, unless
I had believed to see
the goodness of the
LORD in the land of
the living.

Psalm 27:13

But the salvation of
the righteous is of
the LORD: he is their
strength in the time
of trouble.

Psalm 37:39

For the grace of God that bringeth salvation
hath appeared to all men,

Teaching us that, denying ungodliness
and worldly lusts, we should live soberly,
righteously, and godly, in this present
world;

Looking for that blessed hope, and the
glorious appearing of the great God and
our Saviour Jesus Christ;

Who gave himself for us, that he might
redeem us from all iniquity, and purify
unto himself a peculiar people, zealous of
good works.

Titus 2:11–14

Blessed be the God and Father of our Lord Jesus Christ, who hath blessed us with all spiritual blessings in heavenly places in Christ:

According as he hath chosen us in him before the foundation of the world, that we should be holy and without blame before him in love:

Having predestinated us unto the adoption of children by Jesus Christ to himself, according to the good pleasure of his will,

To the praise of the glory of his grace, wherein he hath made us accepted in the beloved.

In whom we have redemption through his blood, the forgiveness of sins, according to the riches of his grace.

Ephesians 1:3–7

A thousand shall fall at thy side, and ten thousand at thy right hand; but it shall not come nigh thee.

Psalm 91:7

And he said unto me, My grace is sufficient for thee: for my strength is made perfect in weakness. Most gladly therefore will I rather glory in my infirmities, that the power of Christ may rest upon me.

2 Corinthians 12:9

But unto every one of us is given grace according to the measure of the gift of Christ.

Ephesians 4:7

72

But the fruit of the Spirit is love, joy, peace,
longsuffering, gentleness, goodness, faith,

Meekness, temperance: against such
there is no law.

And they that are Christ's have crucified
the flesh with the affections and lusts.

If we live in the Spirit, let us also walk in
the Spirit.

Galatians 5:22–25

Wherein he hath
abounded toward us
in all wisdom and
prudence.

Ephesians 1:8

Ye that love the LORD, hate evil: he preserveth the souls of his saints; he delivereth them out of the hand of the wicked.

Light is sown for the righteous, and gladness for the upright in heart.

Rejoice in the LORD, ye righteous; and give thanks at the remembrance of his holiness.

Psalm 97:10–12

Rejoice in the Lord always: and again I say, Rejoice.

Philippians 4:4

Always bearing about in the body the dying of the Lord Jesus, that the life also of Jesus might be made manifest in our body.

For we which live are always delivered unto death for Jesus' sake, that the life also of Jesus might be made manifest in our mortal flesh.

So then death worketh in us, but life in you.

2 Corinthians 4:10–12

Make us glad according to the days wherein thou hast afflicted us, and the years wherein we have seen evil.

Psalm 90:15

Christ hath redeemed us from the
curse of the law, being made a curse
for us: for it is written, Cursed is
every one that hangeth on a tree:

That the blessing of Abraham might
come on the Gentiles through Jesus
Christ; that we might receive the
promise of the Spirit through faith.

Galatians 3:13–14

I waited patiently for the LORD;
and he inclined unto me, and
heard my cry.

Psalm 40:1

For ye were sometimes darkness,
but now are ye light in the Lord:
walk as children of light.

Ephesians 5:8

76

But God, who is rich in mercy, for his great love wherewith he loved us,

Even when we were dead in sins, hath quickened us together with Christ, (by grace ye are saved;)

And hath raised us up together, and made us sit together in heavenly places in Christ Jesus:

That in the ages to come he might shew the exceeding riches of his grace in his kindness toward us through Christ Jesus.

For by grace are ye saved through faith; and that not of yourselves: it is the gift of God:

Not of works, lest any man should boast.

For we are his workmanship, created in Christ Jesus unto good works, which God hath before ordained that we should walk in them.

Ephesians 2:4–10

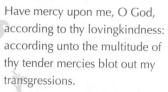

Have mercy upon me, O God, according to thy lovingkindness: according unto the multitude of thy tender mercies blot out my transgressions.

Wash me throughly from mine iniquity, and cleanse me from my sin.

For I acknowledge my transgressions: and my sin is ever before me.

Against thee, thee only, have I sinned, and done this evil in thy sight: that thou mightest be justified when thou speakest, and be clear when thou judgest.

Behold, I was shapen in iniquity; and in sin did my mother conceive me.

Behold, thou desirest truth in the inward parts: and in the hidden

part thou shalt make me to know
wisdom.

Purge me with hyssop, and I shall
be clean: wash me, and I shall be
whiter than snow.

Make me to hear joy and gladness;
that the bones which thou hast
broken may rejoice.

Hide thy face from my sins, and
blot out all mine iniquities.

Create in me a clean heart, O
God; and renew a right spirit within
me.

Cast me not away from thy
presence; and take not thy holy spirit
from me.

Restore unto me the joy of thy
salvation; and uphold me with thy
free spirit.

Psalm 51:1–12

Nevertheless we, according to his promise, look for new heavens and a new earth, wherein dwelleth righteousness.

2 Peter 3:13

Turn us again, O God, and cause thy face to shine; and we shall be saved.

Psalm 80:3

For in him dwelleth all the fulness of the Godhead bodily.

And ye are complete in him, which is the head of all principality and power:

In whom also ye are circumcised with the circumcision made without hands, in putting off the body of the sins of the flesh by the circumcision of Christ:

Buried with him in baptism, wherein also ye are risen with him through the faith of the operation of God, who hath raised him from the dead.

And you, being dead in your sins and the uncircumcision of your flesh, hath he quickened together with him, having forgiven you all trespasses;

Blotting out the handwriting of ordinances that was against us, which was contrary to us, and took it out of the way, nailing it to his cross;

And having spoiled principalities and powers, he made a shew of them openly, triumphing over them in it.

Colossians 2:9–15

Many, O Lord my God, are thy
wonderful works which thou
hast done, and thy thoughts
which are to us-ward: they
cannot be reckoned up in order
unto thee: if I would declare
and speak of them, they are
more than can be numbered.

Psalm 40:5

But my God shall supply all
your need according to his
riches in glory by Christ Jesus.

Philippians 4:19

I have called upon thee, for thou wilt hear me, O
God: incline thine ear unto me, and hear my speech.

Shew thy marvellous lovingkindness, O thou that
savest by thy right hand them which put their trust in
thee from those that rise up against them.

Keep me as the apple of the eye, hide me under
the shadow of thy wings.

Psalm 17:6–8

Giving thanks unto the Father, which
hath made us meet to be partakers of the
inheritance of the saints in light:

Who hath delivered us from the power
of darkness, and hath translated us into the
kingdom of his dear Son:

In whom we have redemption through
his blood, even the forgiveness of sins.

Colossians 1:12–14

Grant thee according
to thine own heart, and
fulfil all thy counsel.

Psalm 20:4

Knowing that he which raised
up the Lord Jesus shall raise
up us also by Jesus, and shall
present us with you.

2 Corinthians 4:14

Be careful for nothing; but in every
thing by prayer and supplication
with thanksgiving let your requests
be made known unto God.

And the peace of God, which
passeth all understanding, shall
keep your hearts and minds
through Christ Jesus.

Philippians 4:6–7

Mine eyes are ever toward
the LORD; for he shall pluck
my feet out of the net.

Psalm 25:15

And every man that
hath this hope in him
purifieth himself,
even as he is pure.

1 John 3:3

Knowing that a man is not
justified by the works of the law,
but by the faith of Jesus Christ,
even we have believed in Jesus
Christ, that we might be justified
by the faith of Christ, and not by
the works of the law: for by the
works of the law shall no flesh
be justified.

Galatians 2:16

Though I walk in the midst of
trouble, thou wilt revive me:
thou shalt stretch forth thine
hand against the wrath of mine
enemies, and thy right hand shall
save me.

The LORD will perfect that
which concerneth me: thy mercy,
O LORD, endureth for ever:
forsake not the works of thine
own hands.

Psalm 138:7–8

We give thanks to God always for you all,
making mention of you in our prayers;

Remembering without ceasing your work
of faith, and labour of love, and patience of
hope in our Lord Jesus Christ, in the sight
of God and our Father;

Knowing, brethren beloved, your
election of God.

For our gospel came not unto you in
word only, but also in power, and in the
Holy Ghost, and in much assurance; as
ye know what manner of men we were
among you for your sake.

And ye became followers of us, and
of the Lord, having received the word
in much affliction, with joy of the Holy
Ghost.

1 Thessalonians 1:2–6

This is the day which the
Lord hath made; we will
rejoice and be glad in it.

Psalm 118:24

For, brethren, ye have
been called unto liberty;
only use not liberty for an
occasion to the flesh, but
by love serve one another.

Galatians 5:13

It is a faithful saying: For if
we be dead with him, we
shall also live with him:

If we suffer, we shall also
reign with him: if we deny
him, he also will deny us.

2 Timothy 2:11–12

For God hath not given us the spirit of
fear; but of power, and of love, and of a
sound mind.

Be not thou therefore ashamed of the
testimony of our Lord, nor of me his
prisoner: but be thou partaker of the
afflictions of the gospel according to
the power of God;

Who hath saved us, and called us
with an holy calling, not according to
our works, but according to his own
purpose and grace, which was given us
in Christ Jesus before the world began.

2 Timothy 1:7–9

The Lord hath done
great things for us;
whereof we are glad.

Psalm 126:3

In whom ye also trusted, after that ye heard the word of truth, the gospel of your salvation: in whom also after that ye believed, ye were sealed with that holy Spirit of promise,

Which is the earnest of our inheritance until the redemption of the purchased possession, unto the praise of his glory.

Ephesians 1:13–14

I called upon the Lord in distress: the Lord answered me, and set me in a large place.

The Lord is on my side; I will not fear: what can man do unto me?

Psalm 118:5–6

For we through the
Spirit wait for the
hope of righteousness
by faith.

Galatians 5:5

He hath not dealt with us
after our sins; nor rewarded us
according to our iniquities.

For as the heaven is high
above the earth, so great is his
mercy toward them that fear
him.

As far as the east is from the
west, so far hath he removed
our transgressions from us.

Psalm 103:10–12

The eyes of your understanding being enlightened; that ye may know what is the hope of his calling, and what the riches of the glory of his inheritance in the saints.

Ephesians 1:18

Behold, what manner of love the Father hath bestowed upon us, that we should be called the sons of God: therefore the world knoweth us not, because it knew him not.

1 John 3:1

The LORD shall preserve thee from all evil: he shall preserve thy soul.

Psalm 121:7

Yea doubtless, and I count all things but
loss for the excellency of the knowledge
of Christ Jesus my Lord: for whom I have
suffered the loss of all things, and do count
them but dung, that I may win Christ,

And be found in him, not having mine
own righteousness, which is of the law, but
that which is through the faith of Christ, the
righteousness which is of God by faith.

Philippians 3:8–9

Thy kingdom is an
everlasting kingdom, and
thy dominion endureth
throughout all generations.

Psalm 145:13

And came and preached
peace to you which were
afar off, and to them that
were nigh.

For through him we both
have access by one Spirit
unto the Father.

Ephesians 2:17–18

Uphold me according unto
thy word, that I may live:
and let me not be ashamed
of my hope.

Hold thou me up, and
I shall be safe: and I will
have respect unto thy
statutes continually.

Psalm 119:116–117

But ye are a chosen
generation, a royal
priesthood, an holy nation,
a peculiar people; that ye
should shew forth the praises
of him who hath called
you out of darkness into his
marvellous light.

1 Peter 2:9

Hear my prayer, O LORD, and
let my cry come unto thee.
Hide not thy face from
me in the day when I am in
trouble; incline thine ear unto
me: in the day when I call
answer me speedily.

Psalm 102:1–2

In whom we have boldness
and access with confidence
by the faith of him.
    Wherefore I desire
that ye faint not at my
tribulations for you, which
is your glory.

Ephesians 3:12–13

Let Israel hope in the LORD:
for with the LORD there is
mercy, and with him is
plenteous redemption.
    And he shall redeem Israel
from all his iniquities.

Psalm 130:7–8

Rejoice not against me, O
mine enemy: when I fall,
I shall arise; when I sit in
darkness, the LORD shall
be a light unto me.

Micah 7:8

Grace and peace be multiplied unto
you through the knowledge of God,
and of Jesus our Lord,

According as his divine power hath
given unto us all things that pertain
unto life and godliness, through the
knowledge of him that hath called us
to glory and virtue:

Whereby are given unto us
exceeding great and precious
promises: that by these ye might be
partakers of the divine nature.

2 Peter 1:2–4

They that sow in tears shall reap in joy.

Psalm 126:5

I, therefore, the prisoner of the Lord, beseech you that
ye walk worthy of the vocation wherewith ye are called.

Ephesians 4:1

Bless the LORD, O my soul: and all that
is within me, bless his holy name.
Bless the LORD, O my soul, and
forget not all his benefits:
Who forgiveth all thine iniquities;
who healeth all thy diseases;
Who redeemeth thy life from
destruction; who crowneth thee with
lovingkindness and tender mercies.

Psalm 103:1–4

Forasmuch as ye know that ye were not
redeemed with corruptible things, as silver
and gold, from your vain conversation
received by tradition from your fathers;

But with the precious blood of Christ,
as of a lamb without blemish and without
spot:

Who verily was foreordained before the
foundation of the world, but was manifest
in these last times for you,

Who by him do believe in God, that
raised him up from the dead, and gave him
glory; that your faith and hope might be in
God.

Seeing ye have purified your souls in
obeying the truth through the Spirit unto
unfeigned love of the brethren, see that
ye love one another with a pure heart
fervently:

Being born again, not of corruptible
seed, but of incorruptible, by the word of
God, which liveth and abideth for ever.

1 Peter 1:18–23

The Lord preserveth the simple: I was brought low, and he helped me.

Return unto thy rest, O my soul; for the Lord hath dealt bountifully with thee.

For thou hast delivered my soul from death, mine eyes from tears, and my feet from falling.

I will walk before the Lord in the land of the living.

Psalm 116:6–9

grow

That we henceforth be no more children, tossed to and fro, and carried about with every wind of doctrine, by the sleight of men, and cunning craftiness, whereby they lie in wait to deceive;

But speaking the truth in love, may grow up into him in all things, which is the head, even Christ.

Ephesians 4:14–15

If thou, LORD, shouldest mark
iniquities, O Lord, who shall stand?
   But there is forgiveness with thee,
that thou mayest be feared.

Psalm 130:3–4

For so is the will of God, that with
well doing ye may put to silence
the ignorance of foolish men:
   As free, and not using
your liberty for a cloke of
maliciousness, but as the servants
of God.

1 Peter 2:15–16

If we confess our sins, he is faithful and just to forgive us our sins, and to cleanse us from all unrighteousness.

1 John 1:9

And be ye kind one to another, tenderhearted, forgiving one another, even as God for Christ's sake hath forgiven you.

Ephesians 4:32

And you, that were sometime alienated
and enemies in your mind by wicked
works, yet now hath he reconciled
   In the body of his flesh through death,
to present you holy and unblameable
and unreproveable in his sight.

Colossians 1:21–22

For finding fault with them,
he saith, Behold, the days
come, saith the Lord, when
I will make a new covenant
with the house of Israel and
with the house of Judah.

Hebrews 8:8

Of his own will begat he
us with the word of truth,
that we should be a kind of
firstfruits of his creatures.

James 1:18

As ye have therefore
received Christ Jesus the
Lord, so walk ye in him.

Colossians 2:6

But after that the kindness and love
of God our Saviour toward man
appeared,
    Not by works of righteousness
which we have done, but according
to his mercy he saved us, by the
washing of regeneration, and
renewing of the Holy Ghost;
    Which he shed on us abundantly
through Jesus Christ our Saviour;
    That being justified by his grace,
we should be made heirs according
to the hope of eternal life.

Titus 3:4–7

If ye then be risen with Christ, seek those things which are above, where Christ sitteth on the right hand of God.

Colossians 3:1

Seeing then that we have a great high priest, that is passed into the heavens, Jesus the Son of God, let us hold fast our profession.

For we have not an high priest which cannot be touched with the feeling of our infirmities; but was in all points tempted like as we are, yet without sin.

Let us therefore come boldly unto the throne of grace, that we may obtain mercy, and find grace to help in time of need.

Hebrews 4:14–16

In the which ye also walked some time, when ye lived in them.

But now ye also put off all these; anger, wrath, malice, blasphemy, filthy communication out of your mouth. Lie not one to another, seeing that ye have put off the old man with his deeds;

And have put on the new man, which is renewed in knowledge after the image of him that created him.

Colossians 3:7–10

The Lord is not slack concerning his promise, as some men count slackness; but is longsuffering to us-ward, not willing that any should perish, but that all should come to repentance.

2 Peter 3:9

Wherein God, willing more abundantly to shew unto the heirs of promise the immutability of his counsel, confirmed it by an oath:

That by two immutable things, in which it was impossible for God to lie, we might have a strong consolation, who have fled for refuge to lay hold upon the hope set before us:

Which hope we have as an anchor of the soul, both sure and stedfast, and which entereth into that within the veil;

Whither the forerunner is for us entered, even Jesus, made an high priest for ever after the order of Melchisedec.

Hebrews 6:17–20

But if we walk in the light, as he is in the light, we have fellowship one with another, and the blood of Jesus Christ his Son cleanseth us from all sin.

1 John 1:7

He that hath an ear, let him hear what the Spirit saith unto the churches; To him that overcometh will I give to eat of the hidden manna, and will give him a white stone, and in the stone a new name written, which no man knoweth saving he that receiveth it.

Revelation 2:17

My flesh and my heart faileth: but God is the strength of my heart, and my portion for ever.

Psalm 73:26

For God so loved the world, that
he gave his only begotten Son, that
whosoever believeth in him should
not perish, but have everlasting life.

John 3:16

The LORD is my strength and my
shield; my heart trusted in him,
and I am helped: therefore my
heart greatly rejoiceth; and with
my song will I praise him.

Psalm 28:7

For his God doth instruct him to
discretion, and doth teach him.

Isaiah 28:26

But this man, after he had offered one
sacrifice for sins for ever, sat down on
the right hand of God;

From henceforth expecting till his
enemies be made his footstool.

For by one offering he hath perfected
for ever them that are sanctified.

Hebrews 10:12–14

My covenant will I not break, nor alter
the thing that is gone out of my lips.

Psalm 89:34

For this God is our God for
ever and ever: he will be
our guide even unto death.

Psalm 48:14

For whatsoever is born of God
overcometh the world: and this
is the victory that overcometh
the world, even our faith.

Who is he that overcometh the
world, but he that believeth that
Jesus is the Son of God?

1 John 5:4–5

He hath remembered his
covenant for ever, the word
which he commanded to a
thousand generations.

Psalm 105:8

And hope maketh not ashamed; because
the love of God is shed abroad in our hearts
by the Holy Ghost which is given unto us.

Romans 5:5

And he that sat upon the throne
said, Behold, I make all things new.
And he said unto me, Write: for
these words are true and faithful.

Revelation 21:5

Our fathers trusted in thee: they
trusted, and thou didst deliver them.

Psalm 22:4

Herein is love, not that we
loved God, but that he loved
us, and sent his Son to be
the propitiation for our sins.

1 John 4:10

This is the covenant that I will make with them after those days, saith the Lord, I will put my laws into their hearts, and in their minds will I write them;

And their sins and iniquities will I remember no more.

Now where remission of these is, there is no more offering for sin.

Having therefore, brethren, boldness to enter into the holiest by the blood of Jesus,

By a new and living way, which he hath consecrated for us, through the veil, that is to say, his flesh;

And having an high priest over the house of God;

Let us draw near with a true heart in full assurance of faith, having our hearts sprinkled from an evil conscience, and our bodies washed with pure water.

Let us hold fast the profession of our faith without wavering; (for he is faithful that promised).

Hebrews 10:16–23

Wherefore seeing we also are compassed about with so great a cloud of witnesses, let us lay aside every weight, and the sin which doth so easily beset us, and let us run with patience the race that is set before us,

Looking unto Jesus the author and finisher of our faith; who for the joy that was set before him endured the cross, despising the shame, and is set down at the right hand of the throne of God.

For consider him that endured such contradiction of sinners against himself, lest ye be wearied and faint in your minds.

Hebrews 12:1–3

Lord, how are they increased that trouble me! many are they that rise up against me.

Many there be which say of my soul, There is no help for him in God. Selah.

But thou, O LORD, art a shield for me; my glory, and the lifter up of mine head.

I cried unto the LORD with my voice, and he heard me out of his holy hill. Selah.

I laid me down and slept; I awaked; for the Lord sustained me.

I will not be afraid of ten thousands of people, that have set themselves against me round about.

Arise, O LORD; save me, O my God: for thou hast smitten all mine enemies upon the cheek bone; thou hast broken the teeth of the ungodly.

Salvation belongeth unto the LORD: thy blessing is upon thy people. Selah.

Psalm 3

Wherefore we receiving a kingdom which
cannot be moved, let us have grace,
whereby we may serve God acceptably
with reverence and godly fear:

For our God is a consuming fire.

Hebrews 12:28–29

Happy is he that hath the God of Jacob for his help,
whose hope is in the LORD his God:

Which made heaven, and earth, the sea, and all that
therein is: which keepeth truth for ever:

Which executeth judgment for the oppressed: which
giveth food to the hungry. The LORD looseth the prisoners:

The LORD openeth the eyes of the blind: the LORD
raiseth them that are bowed down: the LORD loveth the
righteous:

The LORD preserveth the strangers; he relieveth the
fatherless and widow: but the way of the wicked he
turneth upside down.

The LORD shall reign for ever, even thy God, O Zion,
unto all generations. Praise ye the LORD.

Psalm 146:5–10

Blessed are the poor in spirit: for theirs is the kingdom of heaven.

Blessed are they that mourn: for they shall be comforted.

Blessed are the meek: for they shall inherit the earth.

Blessed are they which do hunger and thirst after righteousness: for they shall be filled.

Blessed are the merciful: for they shall obtain mercy.

Blessed are the pure in heart: for they shall see God.

Blessed are the peacemakers: for they shall be called the children of God.

Blessed are they which are persecuted for righteousness' sake: for theirs is the kingdom of heaven.

Blessed are ye, when men shall revile you, and persecute you, and shall say all manner of evil against you falsely, for my sake.

Rejoice, and be exceeding glad: for great is your reward in heaven: for so persecuted they the prophets which were before you.

Matthew 5:3–12

Jesus answered and said unto him,
Verily, verily, I say unto thee, Except
a man be born again, he cannot
enter the kingdom of God.

Nicodemus saith unto him, How
can a man be born when he is old?
can he enter the second time into his
mother's womb, and be born?

Jesus answered, Verily, verily, I say
unto thee, Except a man be born of

water and of the Spirit, he cannot enter into
the kingdom of God.

That which is born of the flesh is flesh; and
that which is born of the Spirit is spirit.

Marvel not that I said unto thee, Ye must
be born again.

The wind bloweth where it listeth, and
thou hearest the sound thereof, but canst not
tell whence it cometh, and whither it goeth:
so is every one that is born of the Spirit.

John 3:5–8

Jesus Christ the same yesterday,
and to day, and for ever.

Hebrews 13:8

Now the God of peace, that brought again
from the dead our Lord Jesus, that great
shepherd of the sheep, through the blood of
the everlasting covenant,

Make you perfect in every good work to
do his will, working in you that which is
wellpleasing in his sight, through Jesus Christ;
to whom be glory for ever and ever. Amen.

Hebrews 13:20–21

Ask, and it shall be given you; seek,
and ye shall find; knock, and it shall
be opened unto you:

For every one that asketh receiveth;
and he that seeketh findeth; and to
him that knocketh it shall be opened.

Matthew 7:7–8

For God sent not his Son into the world to condemn the world; but that the world through him might be saved.

He that believeth on him is not condemned: but he that believeth not is condemned already, because he hath not believed in the name of the only begotten Son of God.

And this is the condemnation, that light is come into the world, and men loved darkness rather than light, because their deeds were evil.

For every one that doeth evil hateth the light, neither cometh to the light, lest his deeds should be reproved.

But he that doeth truth cometh to the light, that his deeds may be made manifest, that they are wrought in God.

John 3:17–21

Therefore I say unto you, Take no thought for your life, what ye shall eat, or what ye shall drink; nor yet for your body, what ye shall put on. Is not the life more than meat, and the body than raiment?

Behold the fowls of the air: for they sow not, neither do they reap, nor gather into barns; yet your heavenly Father feedeth them. Are ye not much better than they?

Which of you by taking thought can add one cubit unto his stature?

And why take ye thought for raiment? Consider the lilies of the field, how they grow; they toil not, neither do they spin:

And yet I say unto you, That even Solomon in all his glory was not arrayed like one of these.

Wherefore, if God so clothe the grass of the field, which to day is, and to morrow is cast into the oven, shall he not much more clothe you, O ye of little faith?

Therefore take no thought, saying, What shall we eat? or, What shall we drink? or, Wherewithal shall we be clothed?

(For after all these things do the Gentiles seek:) for your heavenly Father knoweth that ye have need of all these things.

But seek ye first the kingdom of God, and his righteousness; and all these things shall be added unto you.

Matthew 6:25–33

Lay not up for yourselves treasures
upon earth, where moth and rust doth
corrupt, and where thieves break
through and steal:

But lay up for yourselves treasures in
heaven, where neither moth nor rust
doth corrupt, and where thieves do not
break through nor steal:

For where your treasure is, there will
your heart be also.

Matthew 6:19–21

Give to him that asketh thee,
and from him that would borrow
of thee turn not thou away.

Matthew 5:42

Ye have heard that it hath been said,
Thou shalt love thy neighbour, and
hate thine enemy.

But I say unto you, Love your
enemies, bless them that curse you,
do good to them that hate you, and
pray for them which despitefully use
you, and persecute you;

Matthew 5:43–44

So the last shall be first, and
the first last: for many be
called, but few chosen.

Matthew 20:16

And one of the scribes came, and having heard them reasoning together, and perceiving that he had answered them well, asked him, Which is the first commandment of all?

And Jesus answered him, The first of all the commandments is, Hear, O Israel; The Lord our God is one Lord:

And thou shalt love the Lord thy God with all thy heart, and with all thy soul, and with all thy mind, and with all thy strength: this is the first commandment.

And the second is like, namely
this, Thou shalt love thy neighbour
as thyself. There is none other
commandment greater than these.

And the scribe said unto him,
Well, Master, thou hast said the
truth: for there is one God; and there
is none other but he:

And to love him with all the heart,
and with all the understanding, and
with all the soul, and with all the
strength, and to love his neighbour
as himself, is more than all whole
burnt offerings and sacrifices.

Mark 12:28–34

But Jesus called them unto him,
and said, Ye know that the princes
of the Gentiles exercise dominion
over them, and they that are great
exercise authority upon them.

But it shall not be so among you:
but whosoever will be great among
you, let him be your minister;

And whosoever will be chief
among you, let him be your servant:

Even as the Son of man came
not to be ministered unto, but to
minister, and to give his life a ransom
for many.

Matthew 20:25–28

The light of the body is the eye: if therefore thine eye be single, thy whole body shall be full of light.

Matthew 6:22

No man can serve two masters: for either he will hate the one, and love the other; or else he will hold to the one, and despise the other. Ye cannot serve God and mammon.

Matthew 6:24

If ye then, being evil, know how to give good gifts unto your children, how much more shall your Father which is in heaven give good things to them that ask him?

Matthew 7:11

Ye call me Master and Lord:
and ye say well; for so I am.

If I then, your Lord and
Master, have washed your feet;
ye also ought to wash one
another's feet.

For I have given you an
example, that ye should do as
I have done to you.

Verily, verily, I say unto you,
The servant is not greater than
his lord; neither he that is sent
greater than he that sent him.

If ye know these things,
happy are ye if ye do them.

John 13:13–17

The kingdom of heaven is like to a grain
of mustard seed, which a man took, and
sowed in his field:

Which indeed is the least of all seeds:
but when it is grown, it is the greatest
among herbs, and becometh a tree, so
that the birds of the air come and lodge
in the branches thereof.

Matthew 13:31–32

The kingdom of heaven is
like unto leaven, which a
woman took, and hid in
three measures of meal, till
the whole was leavened.

Matthew 13:33

Then shall the righteous
shine forth as the sun in the
kingdom of their Father. Who
hath ears to hear, let him hear.

Matthew 13:43

The kingdom of heaven is like unto treasure
hid in a field; the which when a man hath
found, he hideth, and for joy thereof goeth and
selleth all that he hath, and buyeth that field.

Matthew 13:44

The kingdom of heaven is like
unto a merchant man, seeking
goodly pearls:
   Who, when he had found
one pearl of great price, went
and sold all that he had, and
bought it.

Matthew 13:45–46

Though I speak with the tongues of men and of angels, and have not charity, I am become as sounding brass, or a tinkling cymbal.

And though I have the gift of prophecy, and understand all mysteries, and all knowledge; and though I have all faith, so that I could remove mountains, and have not charity, I am nothing.

1 Corinthians 13:1–2

Charity suffereth long, and is kind; charity envieth not; charity vaunteth not itself, is not puffed up,

Doth not behave itself unseemly, seeketh not her own, is not easily provoked, thinketh no evil;

Rejoiceth not in iniquity, but rejoiceth in the truth;

Beareth all things, believeth all things, hopeth all things, endureth all things.

Charity never faileth: but whether there be prophecies, they shall fail; whether there be tongues, they shall cease; whether there be knowledge, it shall vanish away.

1 Corinthians 13:4–8

For now we see through a glass, darkly; but then face to face: now I know in part; but then shall I know even as also I am known.

And now abideth faith, hope, charity, these three; but the greatest of these is charity.

1 Corinthians 13:12–13

134

For I know the thoughts that I think
toward you, saith the LORD, thoughts
of peace, and not of evil, to give you
an expected end.

Then shall ye call upon me, and ye
shall go and pray unto me, and I will
hearken unto you.

And ye shall seek me, and find me,
when ye shall search for me with all
your heart.

And I will be found of you, saith
the LORD: and I will turn away your
captivity, and I will gather you from
all the nations, and from all the
places whither I have driven you,
saith the LORD; and I will bring you
again into the place whence I caused
you to be carried away captive.

Jeremiah 29:11–14

Trust in the LORD with
all thine heart; and lean
not unto thine own
understanding.

Proverbs 3:5

Also I heard the voice
of the Lord, saying,
Whom shall I send,
and who will go for us?
Then said I, Here am I;
send me.

Isaiah 6:8

Therefore Eli said unto Samuel,
Go, lie down: and it shall be,
if he call thee, that thou shalt
say, Speak, LORD; for thy servant
heareth. So Samuel went and lay
down in his place.

And the LORD came, and stood,
and called as at other times,
Samuel, Samuel. Then Samuel
answered, Speak; for thy servant
heareth.

1 Samuel 3:9–10

And God is able to make all
grace abound toward you;
that ye, always having all
sufficiency in all things, may
abound to every good work.

2 Corinthians 9:8

And Hannah prayed, and said, My heart rejoiceth in the LORD, mine horn is exalted in the LORD: my mouth is enlarged over mine enemies; because I rejoice in thy salvation.

There is none holy as the LORD: for there is none beside thee: neither is there any rock like our God.

Talk no more so exceeding proudly; let not arrogancy come out of your mouth: for the LORD is a God of knowledge, and by him actions are weighed.

The bows of the mighty men are broken, and they that stumbled are girded with strength.

They that were full have hired out themselves for bread; and they that were hungry ceased: so that the barren hath born seven; and she that hath many children is waxed feeble.

The LORD killeth, and maketh alive: he bringeth down to the grave, and bringeth up.

1 Samuel 2:1–6

And, behold, I come quickly;
and my reward is with me, to
give every man according as
his work shall be.

I am Alpha and Omega, the
beginning and the end, the
first and the last.

Blessed are they that do his
commandments, that they may
have right to the tree of life,
and may enter in through the
gates into the city.

Revelation 22:12–14

Begin or End Your Day with

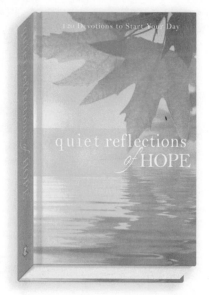

Each new day requires of us only one thing—to put our hand in God's and head out into the world with him as our guide and friend.

Each devotional volume contains 120 devotions with full color

Revell
a division of Baker Publishing Group
www.RevellBooks.com

a Quiet Moment with God

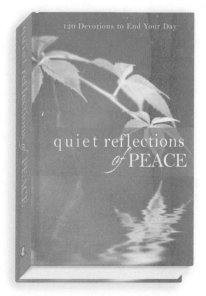

120 Devotions to End Your Day

quiet reflections *of* PEACE

At day's end, God's instructions to us are simple: leave your burdens with him, and rest in his care.

art and attractive, contemporary designs. Great for gift giving!